HALLUCINOGENS

Hallucinogens twist the way users see the world around them.

HALLUCINOGENS

Ann Ricki Hurwitz
Sue Hurwitz

THE ROSEN PUBLISHING GROUP, INC.
NEW YORK

The people pictured in this book are only models; they, in no way, practice or endorse the activities illustrated. Captions serve only to explain the subjects of photographs and do not in any way imply a connection between the real-life models and the staged situations.

Published in 1992 by The Rosen Publishing Group, Inc.
29 East 21st Street, New York, NY 10010

First Edition

Printed in the United States of America.

Library of Congress Cataloging-in-Publication Data

Hurwitz, Ann Ricki
    Hallucinogens / by Ann Ricki Hurwitz and
    Sue Hurwitz. — 1st ed.
    (The Drug Abuse Prevention Library)
    Includes bibliographical references and index.
    Summary: Describes psilocybin, LSD, mescaline, and
    other hallucinogenic drugs and discusses their
    dangerous and destructive effects.
        ISBN 0-8239-1461-5
        1. Hallucinogenic drugs—Juvenile literature.
    [1. Hallucinogenic drugs. 2. Drugs. 3. Drug
    abuse.] I. Hurwitz, Sue, 1934– . II. Title.
    III. Series
    HV5809.5.H87 1992   92-8599
    362.29'4—dc20   CIP
                            AC

Contents

13.16

Introduction

Do you know what hallucinogens are?

Hallucinogens are dangerous drugs. They are illegal. They upset the chemicals in a person's brain. That changes the way the brain works. These drugs affect the user's senses—the way the person thinks, feels, sees, hears, and smells.

People who are high on hallucinogens are called *trippers*. They often claim that colors are brighter, sounds are louder, and odors are stronger.

Hallucinogens cause users to hallucinate—to see and hear things that are not real. Users may also see and hear real things in a confused, dreamlike way. They may "hear" colors and "see" sounds.

Users often seem spaced out. They may not understand time and space in a normal way. When they do not understand things, they do not react normally. Trippers may have trouble speaking. They may have trouble controlling their muscles.

Hallucinogens may cause users to become easily upset, nervous, or depressed. Trippers may lose interest in life, or feel that they have lost control of their lives. They often become dependent on larger doses of drugs.

This book is about hallucinogens. It explains how the drugs can affect your mind. It shows how they may affect the lives of people who use them.

Hallucinogens can injure your mind and your body. Just trying these powerful drugs can make you mentally or physically ill. This book lists places that users can go for help.

These drugs are illegal. They are a dangerous trip to nowhere.

And they are not worth the risk!

Many hallucinogens are made from plants like the peyote cactus.

CHAPTER 1

Hallucinogens— What They Are and What They Do

*T*here are many kinds of drugs. Some are legal and are used to help cure illnesses. Some are illegal and can only harm people. Some drugs are natural; that is, they occur in the world. They are plants, or parts of plants. Other drugs are human-made. They are made in laboratories by scientists. Some human-made drugs are legal and useful. Others are illegal and very dangerous. Hallucinogens fall into the illegal-and-dangerous category.

10 | *Natural Hallucinogens*

Magic Mushrooms

Mushrooms are plants called *fungi*. Fungi live on living or dead plants. Mushrooms grow all around the world. There are thousands of kinds of mushrooms. The kind that you find in grocery stores are safe and are also good for you.

But some mushrooms are poisonous and can kill you. Some mushrooms—called magic mushrooms—contain a chemical called *psilocybin*. This natural chemical is a hallucinogen.

Magic mushrooms may be eaten fresh, cooked, dried, or crushed. Usually they are swallowed in tablets or capsules.

The psilocybin in magic mushrooms causes users to see, hear, and feel things in ways that are not normal. Often users see very colorful hallucinations. They may feel light-headed or so relaxed that nothing seems to matter. Psilocybin may also cause diarrhea and stomach cramps.

The effects of magic mushrooms begin in about 15 minutes and may last 9 hours. Sometimes users have flashbacks.

Mescaline

Peyote is a short, spineless cactus plant. It grows in the deserts of Mexico and the

southwestern United States. The top of
the cactus has a little crown or button.
This button contains a chemical called
mescaline.

Slices of the peyote crown may be eaten
fresh or dried into hard, brown buttons.
The buttons are often swallowed whole or
used to make tea. Peyote buttons can be
kept for many years.

Mescaline can also be made by humans.
Human-made mescaline is most often
found in capsules or tablets.

Mescaline changes the way the brain
works. It causes users to see things, especially
colors, that are not real. Mescaline can
cause hallucinations.

About an hour after using mescaline,
trippers may have physical effects such as
nausea and vomiting. They may have
ragged breathing, increased heart rate, or
the shakes. Sometimes the pupils of the
eyes are dilated, or enlarged. The effects
of mescaline have been known to last up
to 12 hours.

Mescaline, or peyote, has been known
as a mind-changing drug for hundreds of
years. The Aztecs of South America used
peyote in religious ceremonies. Even
today some Native Americans want to use
it in their religious ceremonies.

12 | Marijuana

Marijuana is sometimes called "pot" or "grass." Marijuana is a drug made from the cannabis, or hemp, plant. This plant grows in warm climates all over the world, including the United States.

The cannabis plant contains more than 400 chemicals. Many of the chemicals stay in a user's body for months. *Tetrahydrocannabinol*, or THC, is the chemical in marijuana that is a hallucinogen.

Marijuana may be added to food or brewed into tea. Usually it is smoked in handmade cigarettes called "joints," "sticks," or "reefers." Smoking one joint of marijuana is as harmful as smoking five cigarettes made of tobacco.

Marijuana may injure both the body and the mind. When smoking marijuana, the tripper holds in the smoke as long as possible. That is very harmful to the lungs. Long-term use may cause lung cancer and heart disease. Marijuana is harmful to the white blood cells, which help fight off disease. Many users become sick more often than nonusers.

Marijuana changes the way the brain works. The effects of marijuana begin about 15 to 30 minutes after using it.

Many people suffer serious side effects from taking drugs.

14 Trippers may feel relaxed, drowsy, or happy. They may have mild hallucinations for several hours. When that happens the user is said to be "high," or "stoned."

Some users find it hard to think clearly or to remember things. They may become moody, easily upset, and unable to pay attention. They may talk and giggle more than usual. That makes it hard to learn at school or on the job. Sometimes they have panic reactions and feel that their lives are out of control.

Drugs do not affect everyone the same way. Doctors still do not know all the long-term effects of using marijuana. But doctors do know that long-time users of marijuana often become dependent on it. They need more and more marijuana just to feel normal.

Long-term use of marijuana damages the brain and nervous system. Users may never think in a normal way again.

Human-Made Hallucinogens
LSD

LSD, or *lysergic acid diethylamide*, is sometimes called "acid." LSD is found on a fungus that grows on rye and other grains. It is also one of the most powerful

drugs made by humans. LSD is 100 times
stronger than magic mushrooms. It is
more than 4,000 times stronger than
mescaline.

LSD is a tasteless, colorless, odorless
white powder. It is made into tablets, or
capsules, or a liquid. Liquid LSD can be
swallowed by putting it onto sugar cubes,
gelatin, blotting paper, stamps, or candy.
Acid may also be injected into a vein.

LSD changes the way the brain works.
Usually a user feels the effects 30 to 90
minutes after taking it. The effects can
last up to 12 hours. Taking a dose of LSD
is called "tripping."

The mental effects of LSD are similar to
those of the other hallucinogens, but even
stronger. A tripper may begin to feel several
different emotions at once. There is no
way to tell at the start if it will be a "good
trip" or a "bad trip."

On a bad trip a user's mind may swing
rapidly from one wild emotion to another.
These changes can be frightening and
make users feel helpless. Sometimes users
think they can attempt superhuman or
dangerous things. Sometimes they feel
panic, confusion, anxiety, or that their
lives are out of control.

16   The physical effects of LSD are sweating, loss of appetite, sleeplessness, dry mouth, and the shakes. LSD may also raise the body temperature, heart rate, and blood pressure. The pupils of the eyes may become dilated.

LSD is so powerful that its effects may never leave the mind or body. Doctors think that LSD may injure children born to users. Trippers often have flashbacks years later even if they never use LSD again.

PCP

PCP, or *phencyclidine,* is sometimes called "angel dust" or "killer weed." PCP is the most dangerous hallucinogen. It is also the one most widely used. Trippers often become physically dependent on PCP. Long-term use may cause brain damage.

PCP was developed as a medicine to put people to sleep or to block pain during surgical operations. But doctors soon learned that it causes confusion, hallucinations, anxiety, and even seizures. PCP is *not* a legal drug today.

PCP is made into a pure, white crystal-like powder. It may be swallowed in tablets or capsules, sniffed, or injected.

The only sure way to avoid getting hooked on drugs is to refuse them.

18 Usually, PCP is sprinkled or sprayed on marijuana, tobacco, crushed parsley leaves, or mint leaves. Then it is smoked. PCP cigarettes are called "hot," "mist," or "sherman."

The effects of PCP begin in 2 to 5 minutes, peak in about 20 minutes, and may last 6 hours. It takes 24 to 48 hours to feel normal again. PCP is stored in the fatty tissue of the body, and trippers can have flashbacks months later.

The effects of PCP are not the same with each trip. Users may see and hear things in ways that are not normal and are often scary. They may talk and walk strangely. The senses of touch and pain may be dulled. Regular use of PCP affects a person's memory, concentration, and judgment.

PCP may speed up the nervous system and cause users to become very excited, restless, irritable, or nervous. It may also slow down the nervous system. With large doses trippers may become drowsy, have convulsions, or go into a coma. They also may have heart failure or a stroke.

Other effects of PCP include increased heart rate and blood pressure, flushing, dizziness, blurred vision, sweating, slurred speech, and numbness.

PCP can cause strange, violent behavior |
and extreme mental confusion. Sometimes
trippers think that they have superhuman
powers and die from drowning, burns,
falls from high places, and car accidents.
Users high on PCP often commit violent
crimes.

Many PCP users take overdoses and act
crazy. Their eyes are jumpy and unfocused.
They move like robots and seem spaced
out. When that happens, it is hard to tell a
PCP user from a person who has serious
mental problems.

That is because a person high on PCP
really is mentally ill. You can never be
sure what he or she may do. It is best to
stay away from anyone on a PCP trip.

MDMA

MDMA, also called *ecstasy*, is a drug made
with both LSD and amphetamines.

Amphetamines are drugs that speed up
the way the brain and body work. Amphetamines are also called "speed," "uppers,"
or "pep pills." They help users feel more
alert. But they are very dangerous drugs.

Because ecstasy contains both LSD and
amphetamines, it is even more harmful
than either one alone.

Hallucinogens can cause violent and unpredictable changes in mood.

Ecstasy is made in illegal labs, so users never can be sure what is in the pills or capsules they buy. The effects of ecstasy are similar to those of LSD. Many times users really get LSD when they pay for ecstasy.

Besides hallucinations, ecstasy may cause depression, nervousness, nausea, and vomiting. The effects of ecstasy begin about 30 minutes after use and may last 4 hours. Like most hallucinogens, ecstasy often causes negative reactions rather than positive ones. Users may never know in advance how their bodies will react to the drugs they take.

Because drugs can change coordination and muscle control, users are more likely to cause serious accidents or injuries.

CHAPTER 2

Some Who Said Yes

Roz liked her new middle school. She liked her classes and most of her teachers. But best of all she liked the new friends she made there.

"Some of us are going to the mall tomorrow for lunch and a movie," Holly told Roz one Friday. "Want to come along?"

"Sure!" Roz said. "What time?"

"Meet us under the big clock at eleven," Holly instructed. "Do you need a ride?"

"No. My sister, Barbara, will drop me."

Roz arrived at the mall early because Barbara was in a hurry to visit her friends.

24 So Roz waited and waited. But Holly and the others did not show up. Just as she was about to leave, the three girls finally arrived.

"I'm sorry we're late," Holly apologized. "But wait until you see what we brought!"

Roz was not sure what Holly meant by the remark, but she didn't say anything. She was relieved to see them.

"Let's get pizza," Gail suggested with a giggle.

"Good idea!" Mavis agreed. "A mushroom pizza!"

"Is that okay with you?" Holly asked Roz with a smile.

"Sure. I love pizza," Roz said.

After the girls ordered a large mushroom pizza and Cokes, Holly turned to Roz. "We were late because we were waiting for Connie. Connie brings us our magic mushrooms."

Roz watched Holly take a plastic bag of crushed, diced mushrooms from her purse. She held them in her lap after showing them to Roz.

"What's magic about them?" Roz asked. "I don't believe in magic."

"Believe me, these mushrooms are magic!" Holly insisted. "They will help you see gorgeous pictures in your mind.

You will see colors you never even imagined! By the time we get to the movie, you'll feel as if you are on another planet."

Roz remembered reading about drugs. Some people got bad side effects the first time they tried drugs. Yet that probably would not happen to her.

The server brought their pizza, and each girl lifted a large slice onto her plate. Holly then sprinkled some of the magic mushrooms onto her slice of pizza. Then she passed the bag to Gail. Gail did the same and handed the bag to Mavis.

But when Mavis passed the bag, Roz paused before opening it. She knew she should say no and pass it on without using any of the drug.

"Go ahead, try some!" Mavis encouraged. "Don't be stupid."

Stupid? Roz always thought kids who used drugs were stupid. But she had never been tempted before.

"Aren't you curious?" Holly asked.

"Yes, I am curious," Roz admitted. "But I've never used drugs before."

"Then it's high time you started!" Gail exclaimed. "Everyone does it!"

Roz knew that was not true. Barbara did not use drugs. And Barbara had many friends.

26

"Make up your mind," Mavis insisted. "It's no big deal."

So Roz said yes. She sprinkled some of the magic mushrooms onto her slice.

"They don't have any taste," she said to Holly. "I'm surprised."

"There's too much other stuff on the pizza to taste *our* mushrooms. But you'll feel the effects soon."

As they walked to the movie, Roz did feel the effects of the magic mushrooms. She got diarrhea! She needed to stop in the restroom twice. She almost didn't make it the second time.

Later, during the movie, Roz had sharp stomach pains. She waited to see the beautiful colors. But instead, the film looked far away and out of focus.

Roz felt sick. She did not care what her friends thought. She wanted to go home before she really embarrassed herself. She turned to tell Holly that she was leaving, but Holly was sound asleep. Gail and Mavis were sleeping, too.

Roz found a telephone in the lobby. She asked a woman standing nearby to dial the number for her. Roz did not say that the numbers looked small enough to dance on the head of a pin. Instead, she lied and said she had lost her glasses.

Drugs make it hard for you to focus on anything that needs concentration.

28 | Barbara was not happy to change her plans. But after Roz explained that she was ill, her sister agreed to pick her up.

Roz waited outside the mall for Barbara. She thought about the magic mushrooms and her new friends. All three of them now were sleeping through the movie.

How could they see gorgeous colors? How could they get any benefits from the drug? They used magic mushrooms and risked bad side effects for nothing.

Was that stupid or what?

When Barbara drove up, Roz did not recognize the car. She knew their car was white, and this one was three shades of orange and four shades of green. All of them gross! The car also looked as big as a bus!

"Come on, Roz," Barbara called. "I haven't got all day to drive you around!"

So Roz slowly made her way to the car.

"What is wrong with you?" Barbara asked. "You look awful!"

"I feel awful, too," Roz replied.

I said yes when I should have said no, she thought to herself. I was even more stupid than the others. But I will not make that mistake next time!

I will never say yes to drugs again!

Carlo Said Yes to Mescaline

Carlo loved horses. Three years ago, when he was 12, he began working on his uncle's ranch. He fed the horses early, gave them water, and brushed them down.

Carlo often went riding after he finished work. Midnight was his favorite horse. Carlo would ride Midnight to the far end of the ranch. He loved feeling the wind against his face. He loved the fresh smell of the air. And he loved being outdoors!

Sometimes Carlo took along a sleeping bag and spent the night out under the stars. He enjoyed that most of all.

Carlo's uncle hired a new ranch hand named Ken. Ken was 17. Carlo and Ken soon became friends. Sometimes they rode together after work.

"Want to try some peyote before we ride out?" Ken asked one day. "Peyote will give you beautiful visions...you will see things in new ways."

Carlo thought about the land, the grass, the flowers, the trees, the hills, and the stream where Midnight stopped to drink. Could that really look any more beautiful than it already did?

"I don't know," Carlo hedged. "I don't do drugs."

Appreciating the world's natural beauty is one way to feel great.

"Why not?" Ken asked. "The effects of mescaline last a long time. You don't need to use it more than once when you want to trip. Live a little, Carlo! Don't be so uptight!"

Carlo said no. But later he wondered what he might be missing. When he and Ken unrolled their sleeping bags, Ken tempted him again.

"I'm starting to see visions," Ken said. "Do you want a peyote button or not?"

Carlo knew he should refuse again. But perhaps once would not hurt. It had been nearly an hour since Ken took the peyote, and nothing had happened to him.

"Yes," Carlo agreed. "Give me a button." Carlo took a swig of water from his canteen to wash down the drug. Then he stretched out on his sleeping bag and waited. And waited.

Carlo stared up at the stars as he usually did. But soon the stars looked different. They glittered more brightly. They seemed bigger and closer. In fact, the stars seemed to be dropping down from the sky onto Carlo's face!

Carlo shut his eyes for a minute. When he opened them, he "saw" giant clouds swallow up the stars. The clouds were dark and scary. They were hanging down

A true friend will try to help another who is on drugs.

lower and lower. Soon they would smother him!

Carlo sat up. He ran to a nearby tree and climbed onto a branch. He began throwing leaves into the air.

"What are you doing?" Ken asked.

"I am shooting scuds at those clouds!" Carlo yelled. "Those clouds have poisonous gas. Can't you smell their terrible odor? Those clouds are trying to kill me!"

"You are having hallucinations," Ken said. "The best way to deal with a bad trip is to try to relax and calm down. Come down and try to sleep your bummer off!"

"No!" Carlo threw a handful of leaves at Ken. "You're after me too! Stay away!"

"Suit yourself," Ken said. He rolled over and studied the bright greens in a blade of grass. He had his own visions to deal with!

Carlo panicked. Could he escape from those deadly clouds? Would the clouds poison him? He wished he could think more clearly. But he felt like puking. And he was trembling so badly that he knew he could not hang onto the tree much longer.

Finally Carlo "saw" a wide river flowing under the tree. Now he could escape! He would jump into the river and swim away.

Carlo jumped.

34   He woke up in the hospital with two broken legs and a huge bump on his head. He ached all over. But he was lucky. He was alive! And he probably would be able to walk. But the doctors were not sure if he would ever be able to ride again.

"I hope you have learned not to mess with drugs." Carlo's uncle said.

"I've learned the hard way," Carlo quietly answered. "I don't need drugs to help me see beautiful things. The world is beautiful just as it is. I'll never say yes to drugs again!"

Nikki Said Yes to Marijuana

Nikki and Robin lived next door to each other and were good friends. They went nearly everywhere together. Nikki was quiet and shy around people she did not know well. Robin was more outgoing and made new friends easily.

Both girls turned 17 and got their driver's licenses. The following weekend they went to a school basketball game. Nikki drove.

During the game Robin began talking to several older girls who sat by them. Mona, one of their new friends, invited Nikki and Robin to a party at her house after the game.

Nikki and Robin accepted. After all, what possibly could happen? Nikki had her parents' car for the evening. If the party was dull they would not even need to call home for a ride. They could just leave.

"Mona said the refreshments are big submarine sandwiches and beer," Robin told Nikki later as they drove to the party. "But I'm sure they'll have soft drinks, too."

"Don't be so sure," Nikki replied. "We don't know Mona that well. It's hard to guess what she and her friends may do."

"So we'll see," Robin answered. "If the party is in the fast lane, we'll just leave."

"Agreed!" Nikki replied.

When Nikki and Robin got to the party they were impressed. There were more boys than girls—for a change! And everyone seemed friendly.

"I'm Garth," said a cute guy standing by the refreshments. "Can I get you something to drink?"

"Do you have soda?" Robin asked. "Yes, what do you want in it?" Garth smiled.

"A few ice cubes would be great," Nikki replied. She picked up a paper plate and reached for a sandwich.

"We can do better than that!" Garth boasted. "How about a little vodka?"

36

"No, thanks," Robin replied.

"I'll pass,too," Nikki told Garth. She took the soda and balanced it on the edge of her plate while Robin got a sandwich. Then both girls looked around for a place to sit.

"Most of these guys are seniors," Robin said between sips of her soda. "I've seen them at school."

"Yeah," Nikki agreed. "And every one of them is cute!"

"Having a good time?" Mona asked as she weaved her way through the crowd.

"The sandwiches are delicious," Robin answered.

"This is Garth and Dino," Mona said. She casually introduced them to each other. "Have fun."

Garth sat down beside Nikki. Dino sat down on the other side of Robin. Garth talked about school and discussed his plans for college. Nikki was glad to listen. Then he asked her to dance.

Nikki was having a great time. Garth was a good dancer. After the first few minutes she did not even feel awkward. But she did get tired and needed to catch her breath. So they sat out the next few dances.

Teens often start smoking because of peer pressure.

38   Garth lit up a joint and offered Nikki a drag. "Want some grass?"

"No, thanks," Nikki said. "I tried pot once when I was about 12. It didn't do anything for me."

"Your grass probably didn't have much THC in it," Garth explained. He looked at the joint in his hand. "This stuff is super! Today's marijuana has more THC. It can really make you feel good!"

Garth put the joint up to Nikki's lips. "Go ahead," he urged. "Take a drag."

Nikki knew she should say no again. But she liked Garth. She hoped he would ask her for a date. She didn't want him to think she was a baby. Besides, she had tried pot before and nothing bad had happened.

So Nikki said yes and inhaled deeply. She held in the smoke as long as she could. Then she let it escape slowly from her lips. She felt like coughing, but instead she cleared her throat.

After Garth finished the joint, he and Nikki began dancing again.

Now Nikki felt as if she were walking through a dream. Everything Garth said seemed so funny that she could not stop giggling. She kept stepping on Garth's toes and giggling even more.

"My feet seem to have a mind of their own," Nikki said. "Are you sure you didn't spike my soda with alcohol?"

"It's the pot," Garth insisted. "It's making you feel slightly drunk."

"Umm," Nikki said. "I didn't think anyone could get *slightly* drunk."

When the record ended, Robin came over to Nikki. "We should leave now," she insisted. "It's getting late."

"Okay," Nikki said. "Goodbye, Garth."

"I'll call you, Nikki," Garth promised.

As they walked to the car Robin said, "Give me your car keys. I'll drive."

"Forget it," Nikki snapped back. "I'm perfectly capable of driving!"

"Look, Nikki," Robin said. "I saw you smoke pot. I know you're high. Your reflexes are so affected that you could hardly dance! Let me drive."

"We are only 10 blocks from home," Nikki pouted. "Nothing will happen."

Nikki got behind the wheel and started the car. As she pulled away from the curb she almost sideswiped several parked cars.

"Some people don't know how to park!" she complained to Robin. She did not say that the cars looked blurry and their shapes seemed to keep changing.

Drugs change the way you experience reality and make it very dangerous to do things that require good judgment.

"Let me drive, Nikki," Robin urged. "I'll be careful with your parents' car."

"I can do it," Nikki insisted. "We'll be there in a few minutes!"

Nikki tried to stop when they came to a traffic light. But her foot could not find the brake pedal. Nikki drove through the red light.

They were hit by a car that started across the intersection on the green light.

Brakes squealed. Cars twisted around each other. Glass broke and flew. Blood splattered. Bones were crushed. The cries of pain were heard everywhere.

Robin ended up in the hospital with seven broken ribs.

But Nikki never regained consciousness. She was dead on arrival at the hospital.

"Nikki should never have said yes to marijuana," Robin moaned between sobs to her parents. "Nikki was my friend . . . she was a good person. She just made a foolish mistake."

Pete Said Yes to LSD

When Pete was 16 he started to hang out with a crowd that used alcohol and drugs. So he began using them, too.

42   Pete and his friend, Logan, often used acid after work. But one night Logan had a bad trip. He insisted that he could stop traffic by pushing cars back with his bare hands.

Pete begged Logan not to try it, but Logan would not listen. Logan claimed that he was more powerful than Superman.

Pete had a bad case of the shakes and felt confused. His heart was pounding. The sound of his heartbeat throbbed in his ears. He felt that his life was out of control. How did he know what Logan could do? Maybe Logan did have special powers.

Logan stepped out into a busy street and shouted for Pete to follow him. When Pete stepped off the curb, he fell. As he struggled to get up from the gutter, Pete heard the thunder of a truck's wheels. He glanced up and saw a big 18-wheeler roaring toward Logan.

"Look out!" Pete shouted as he slowly staggered to his feet. But Logan did not hear him. He was too busy trying to control traffic.

Pete watched as Logan stood tall with both hands thrust out before him. The truck driver slammed on his brakes and leaned on his horn. But Logan did not move an inch.

Until he was hit by the truck.

Logan was killed instantly. Right before Pete's eyes. Pete was horrified. He felt guilty about Logan's death.

Pete felt so guilty that he gave up drugs and alcohol. He gave up his old friends. He was determined to make something of himself. He took his schoolwork seriously and studied hard. Eventually Pete made friends who did not do drugs.

Now Pete was 18. He had turned his life around. He would soon graduate from high school. He had earned a scholarship to go to college. He and his new girlfriend, Heather, were in love.

But three days before graduation Pete's past came back to haunt him. He had an LSD flashback.

Pete and Heather were standing by the stair railing on the third floor of the school. They were talking about their date that evening when Pete freaked out.

All of a sudden he began to sweat and tremble. He felt confused. He "heard" a voice that said he could do anything.

"Watch me, Heather!" Pete bragged. "I will fly down to the first floor!"

"You're kidding, right?" Heather asked. She could not imagine what had happened to Pete. Why was he acting so weirdly?

44 | He even looked different. The pupils of his eyes were dilated, and he had a funny expression on his face.

"No! I am not kidding." Pete threw his books on the floor and stretched out his arms. "Watch me soar through the air!" He gave Heather a wink. "But I will fly right back to you."

"Don't, Pete!" Heather screamed.

But Pete climbed up on the railing and tried to fly off of it.

Heather did not hear Pete hit the floor below. Her mind blocked that out. But she saw his body sprawled out from the fall. She thought he was dead.

By the time Heather ran down the stairs a crowd had gathered. As she pushed her way through she heard Pete moan. Heather cried with relief. Pete was alive!

"Call an ambulance!" someone yelled.

"Don't move him!" someone else advised.

Heather sat on the floor beside Pete. She took his hand and held it tightly. Finally Pete opened his eyes.

"I must have had an LSD flashback," Pete told Heather in a soft, halting voice. "I'm sorry."

Pete was not able to attend graduation. He was not able to use his scholarship. Pete spent three months in the hospital

The rise in drug use in America has also caused a sharp rise in the country's crime rate. Most of this crime is committed by users who need to support their habit.

46 with a broken back. He spent another year in therapy before he could move around without his wheelchair.

"You paid a terrible price for doing drugs," Heather often told Pete when she visited him.

At first Pete was so weak that he only nodded in answer. But after he got better he could talk.

"I was foolish to say yes to drugs." Pete admitted. "I was drug-free for years, but you are never free again once you do drugs!"

Molly Said Yes to PCP

Both of Molly's parents had to work long hours. Molly was often at home alone. When she was younger, she played outside with other kids in the neighborhood. But now she spent more time inside watching TV or doing her homework.

Molly's older brother, Marco, was 17. Marco was not at home much. When he was at home he was busy with his buddies. On weekends he and his friends often did drugs on the back porch.

When Molly turned 12, Marco gave her a drag off his PCP joint as a birthday present.

Molly became very excited and started acting crazy. She climbed onto the swing that hung from a tree and started doing dangerous stunts. Molly fell off the swing many times and scraped her arms and knees. But she did not feel any pain, so she let her wounds bleed and kept showing off.

After that, Molly joined her brother and his friends when they smoked joints laced with PCP. Soon she became hooked.

Molly began having trouble at school. She could not think straight or remember things. She often got mad at her teachers and was very rude. Her classmates also got on her nerves. Molly would push them out of the way when she walked down the halls. Everyone began to avoid Molly.

The school principal sent a letter to Molly's parents requesting a conference, and her mother was furious.

"Are you in some kind of trouble?" she asked, showing Molly the letter.

"No," Molly replied. "It's just that the teachers don't like me. They're on my case for nothing!"

Molly's mother asked a school counselor to have a phone conference since she could not get time off from work.

"The counselor told Mother that you are moody and rude and failing most of your

Sudden failing grades are sometimes a sign of drug use.

classes," Molly's father reported. "You're grounded until you straighten this out!"

Grounded? Molly almost laughed. She did not have any friends to run around with anymore. They had all dropped her. And she did not care. When she was not smoking PCP with Marco and his buddies, she slept. So what if she was grounded?

Molly knew she should lay off the drugs for a while and pay more attention to her schoolwork. But it was too late. She could not get through the week without her PCP at least every other day.

Molly was not quite 13, and she was sick of always being on the wrong side of the rules. First at school, and now at home. Maybe she needed help. Maybe she should tell her mom. But her dad would kill her if he knew she did drugs!

One weekend Marco and his friends and Molly were high on PCP. The boys began arguing about getting money for more drugs. They punched each other around. One of them pulled a knife and cut Marco on the arm. They complained that Molly did not do her share to bring in money. Then they told her that they were going to rob a gas station at midnight and she had to come along.

50   "I didn't know you broke the law to buy drugs," Molly told Marco. "Why didn't you tell me before?"

"Don't worry, Molly. I'll take care of it," Marco insisted. "I don't want you to get involved in this."

"But I am involved!" Molly pouted. "I want to help!"

Molly was sent into the gas station to buy a bag of chips. She was pretty nervous, and she felt a little dizzy. But she was fearless. She felt as if she could handle the robbery all by herself if necessary.

When Molly went to the check out, the manager rang up her purchase. While the cash register was open, Marco and two of his friends burst through the door and demanded money.

The station manager set off an alarm, and the noise sent Marco into a rage. Marco started spraying the room with bullets. He yelled something, but his words were slurred. Molly could not tell if he was talking to her or trying to scare the manager. Marco shot the manager just as the manager drew a pistol and shot Marco.

"Come, on," the boys shouted at Molly as they ran out the door. "Leave him!"

Small crimes, like stealing from home, often lead drug users to larger crimes that support their growing habit.

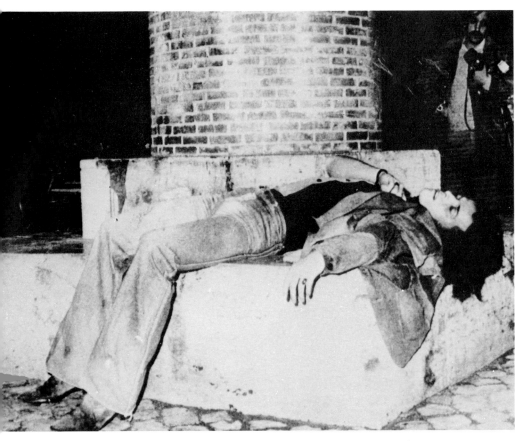

Many drug users lose control of their lives.

But Molly was horrified. She could not leave her brother dying on the floor. She bent down and held Marco's head in her lap. She kept calling his name. When the police arrived they had to pull a screaming Molly away from her dead brother.

Molly's father later told her that she had been fingerprinted and had spent the night in jail. But Molly did not remember any of it. The last thing she remembered was the look in Marco's eyes when he went into that rage.

Molly even blocked out most of the time she spent in the hospital and later in the halfway house. Because of her age, Molly was not sent to prison, but she now had a criminal record.

By the time Molly straightened out her problems with the law she was 14. And she felt rotten. Because she was still on probation, she had to live at home. And she had to go to school. Molly was so depressed that she wanted to stop living.

Marco was dead. His friends were in prison. Molly felt guilty, too. She had no friends of her own. Her parents blamed her for Marco's death, and they did not talk to her. Big deal! They were never home anyway! Now the only person Molly ever saw was her parole officer.

Molly hated her life. She slept through most of her classes. When she did stay awake, she got into trouble with other students or with her teachers. She spent more time waiting outside the principal's office than she did in the classroom.

Molly simply couldn't cope with her life without drugs.

54   But she needed money to buy drugs. So Molly began selling her body to get money for drugs. She knew that sleeping around was as dangerous as doing drugs. But by now she did not care. She had absolutely no self-respect. Her self-image could not have been lower if she had pulled the gun and shot Marco herself.

Molly looked up some of Marco's old friends. They sold her drugs. When they could not get PCP, she bought whatever they had. They often sold her ecstasy, which they claimed was even better than PCP. She did not care what she used as long as it kept her from thinking about her problems and her life.

Molly soon overdosed. Was it on purpose? Or did the drugs she bought poison her?

Molly was 14 when she died. She had used PCP for two years and other drugs for about three months. She did not want to say yes again to drugs. But she did not have the courage to say no.

Molly was so confused that she did not even try to get help. She could have gone to a clinic or a hospital for therapy to help kick her drug habit. She could have asked for help at school. She could have asked her parents to help her. Her friends might have kept her from feeling so lonely, if she had had any friends.

But Molly could not think clearly. She could not see an end to the mess her life had become. Molly became one of a huge number of people who die from using drugs every year.

Molly let drugs destroy her life.

Parents, teachers, friends, and counselors are just a few of the people who can help teens work out their problems.

CHAPTER 3

Know the Facts

*D*octors always look for new drugs to help people. But now doctors know that the effects of hallucinogens are harmful and unpredictable. They know that different people have different reactions to drugs. Doctors also know that heavy use of hallucinogens can cause mental illness and brain damage. Therefore, using hallucinogens is *always* against the law.

You can never be sure what is in illegal drugs. Hallucinogens sold today are dangerous, and using them may be fatal. Sometimes even one dose can kill. Yet it is possible that you may not have a bad trip the first time or two that you try a drug.

58   But even if you get short-term pleasure and feel good and forget your worries, you are harming yourself. Becoming dependent on illegal drugs is like making yourself handicapped.

Do you really want to injure your mind and your body? Do you want to be a slave to flashbacks? Do you want to be a slave to drug dealers? Do you want to risk being on the wrong side of the law?

Do you really need these problems in your life?

Think about those questions. Ask yourself if hallucinogens could possibly be worth what they may cost you. Remember that *all* drugs are poisons if used in large enough amounts.

Then decide what is best for you.

Help List

Associations

- National Institute on Drug Abuse (NIDA)
  NIDA Information and Treatment Center
  12280 Wilkens Avenue
  Rockville, MD 20852
  Hotline: 1-800-662-HELP

- National Council on Alcoholism and Drug
    Dependency
  12 West 21st Street
  New York, NY 10010
  24-Hour Hotline: 1-800-622-2255

- National Prevention Network
  444 North Capitol Street NW
  Washington, D.C. 20001

- American Council for Drug Education
  204 Monroe Street
  Rockville, MD 20850
  (302) 294-0600

- Narcotics Anonymous
  World Service Office
  16155 Wyandotte Street
  Van Nuys, CA 91406

Hotlines

- 1-800-662-HELP
  National Institute on Drug Abuse
  Information and Referral Line
  Monday through Friday
  8:30 A.M.–4:30 P.M.

- 1-800-554-KIDS
  National Federation of Parents for Drug-Free Youth
  Monday through Friday
  9:00 A.M.–5:00 P.M.

Glossary

Explaining New Words

amphetamine Drug that speeds up the functions of the brain and body.

bummer A bad experience, or "bad trip," from using a drug.

hallucinogen Drug that upsets the chemicals in the brain, causing the user to see, hear, smell, and behave differently.

high The effects of a hallucinogen on the user.

hooked State of being addicted to a drug.

LSD Lysergic acid diethylamide, a strong human-made hallucinogenic drug.

MDMA Human-made hallucinogenic drug containing a mix of both LSD and amphetamines; also called *ecstasy*.

magic mushroom Mushroom (fungus) containing *psilocybin*, a hallucinogen.

mescaline Natural chemical that is a hallucinogen; found in the peyote cactus plant.

overdose Too much of a drug, causing sickness or death.

PCP Phencyclidine, the most dangerous human-made hallucinogen.

peyote Cactus plant whose top "button" contains mescaline, a hallucinogenic drug.

psilocybin Natural chemical that is a hallucinogenic drug found in "magic mushrooms."

THC Tetrahydrocannabinol, a common hallucinogenic chemical found in marijuana.

tripper A person who has upset the chemicals in his or her brain by using a drug.

For Further Reading

Algeo, Philippa. *Acid and Hallucinogens*. New York: Franklin Watts, 1990.

Anonymous. *Go Ask Alice*. New York: Simon & Schuster, 1971.

Berger, Gilda. *Addiction*. New York: Franklin Watts, 1982.

Condon, Judith. *The Pressure to Take Drugs*. New York: Franklin Watts, 1990.

Levy, Stephen J., Ph.D. *Managing the Drugs in Your Life*. New York: McGraw-Hill, 1983.

Shulman, Jeffrey. *Focus on Hallucinogens*. Frederick, Maryland: Twenty-First Century Books, 1991.

———. *The Drug-Alert Dictionary and Resource Guide*.

Woods, Geraldine. *Drug Use and Drug Abuse*. New York: Franklin Watts, 1986.

Index

About the Authors

Ann Ricki Hurwitz holds a BA in Linguistics from the University of Colorado. Sue Hurwitz holds an MA in Education from the University of Missouri. They are coauthors of eighteen short stories and a social studies textbook for young adults.

Photo Credits

Cover photo: Stuart Rabinowitz
Photos on pages 2, 17, 20, 22, 27, 32, 48, 51, 56: Dru Nadler;
page 8: Photo Researchers, Inc. © Allan D. Cruickshank;
pages 13, 37, 40: Stuart Rabinowitz; page 30: Mary Lauzon;
pages 45, 52: AP/Wide World Photos.

Design & Production: Blackbirch Graphics, Inc.